AF584011

I am a Yiman woman from Central Queensland. The Yiman are one of the First Peoples of the Taroom area in Central Queensland. Our people were great hunters and warriors who travelled South to the Bunya gatherings with many other nations. We ate bunya nuts for many weeks. The first white man to explore our nation was Ludwig Leichardt. We helped him travel through our area. He stayed with our people as he moved North. We were friendly and helped him. And then the new people arrived and it became a war with our people. This war was over our land and who could use it. It was also over who could take the food from the land and the water. It was a very bad time for my people!

My nine siblings and I were born in Rockhampton in Central Queensland. This story is about my Nana who lived near the Dawson Ranges in Central Queensland. My Nana was a Yiman woman from Taroom on the Dawson River. The Dawson River was where my Nana got food and water. It was a wonderful and special place for my Nana. My Nana was moved from Taroom and forced to walk, carrying her baby, my mother, over 210 kilometres to Woorabinda. This was called a Mission which the white superintendents had built to house our people. My Nana had to stay in this Mission!

One day, my Nana heard that the children who were called half-caste were being taken away to a dormitory to live. The children who may have had a white father were called half-caste. My Mum had brown skin because my great grandmother married a Chinaman who lived in the Taroom area. He was employed to build the roads with bricks at the time.

My Nana was very scared that they would take her daughter and fourteen other children away too! The children were going to be kept away from their mothers and fathers in the dorm house which had high fences all around it. One day, the white superintendents came looking for the brown-coloured children to take them away! The older women of the camp quickly painted the children's skin with charcoal to hide their skin colour. They rolled the brown-coloured children in the dirt, fat and charcoal from the fire. The children were very black and dirty when the superintendents saw them. By the grace of God, my mother and her siblings were never taken from my grandmother, unlike the children from many other families. This is a photo of my mother, Marcia Hassall.

The mountains to the South and West of Woorabinda are the Dawson Ranges. Nana lived at Woorabinda in a bark hut called a humpy. The humpy was located away from the dorms. My mother lived together with her siblings and Nana in this humpy.

The bark that was used to build the humpy was very strong. It was cut into long strips like sheets of roof steel. The bark was then put over the top of poles to form our house. It worked very well at stopping the water and the wind. Nana had a dirt floor and she cooked on an outside fire. Nana did not have any money for food and almost all her food came from the bush and the ground. The only other foods she received were rations of tea, flour and sugar. This came from the Government.

They hunted for food in the bush. There was plenty of food to eat there, like kangaroos, emu, goannas and small animals. In the soil, they found berries, yams, and other bulbs which they ate. They made a vegetable garden and grew their own food as well. The bush provided meat and plants to eat. The streams and creeks provided water for drinking, and the vegetable garden gave them food as well. The food was cooked on a fire at night. The fire was made from wood that was collected in the bush. They lived off the land!

The Dawson area has beautiful bush with creeks and rocks. During this time, there were no farms, or other people in the mountains. There were only animals and plants. It was not good land for sheep or cattle grazing, so it was left as bush. The land was steep in places and the eucalypt trees grew everywhere. This was my family's home.

Being with your father, mother, sisters, brothers, aunties and uncles is very important in our family. I thought of all those children who were taken away from their family and the struggle they would have had. At the time when the children were separated, they were made to live like white people. They were also forbidden to speak their own language. But did those children forget their families? No! Not for one minute!

Central Queensland has lots of special things to see. It has big fat trees called bottle trees and big forests. Today there are large areas of fruit and other trees. The ground is full of rich minerals and energy. Many people visit the Carnarvon Gorge and the National Park which is close to where I still live. One day, Central Queensland may be the food bowl for people all over the world. It is a special, rich, and beautiful place on Earth.

Nowadays, the community re-enacts the walk from Taroom to Woorabinda. They walk more than 210 kilometres from the former Taroom Aboriginal Mission to the Central Queensland community of Woorabinda. Some people say that our family is blessed to stay together, but in our hearts, we give thanks to God for keeping us together. I am very thankful to God for this blessing.

Word bank

Yiman
Queensland
Woorabinda
warriors
Bunya
gatherings
Ludwig
Leichardt
Taroom
siblings
Rockhampton
superintendents
Mission
half-caste
dormitory
Chinaman
brown-coloured
charcoal
humpy
Government
kangaroos
emu
goannas
vegetable
Carnarvon Gorge
beautiful
grazing
eucalypt
struggle
separated
forbidden
language
community
re-enacts
Aboriginal
minerals
energy